MALDIVES TRAVEL GUIDE 2024

Your Ultimate handbook for an unforgettable journey

CORY R. HOBBS

Copyright © 2023 [Cory R. Hobbs]

All rights reserved. Except for brief quotations included in critical reviews and certain other noncommercial uses allowed by copyright law, no part of this publication may be reproduced, distributed, or transmitted in any form or by any means, including photocopying, recording, or other electronic or mechanical methods, without the prior written permission of the copyright holder.

TABLE OF CONTENTS

Chapter one..**5**
   Introduction... 5
Chapter two..**14**
   Planning your trip... 14
Chapter three...**27**
   Getting Around...27
Chapter four...**35**
   Accommodations... 35
Chapter five..**43**
   Activities and Attractions.......................................43
Chapter six..**57**
   Local Cuisine... 57
Chapter seven...**66**
   Health and safety..66
Chapter eighth..**75**
   Shopping and souvenirs....................................... 75
Chapter nine...**84**
   Nightlife and Entertainment................................. 84
Chapter ten...**92**
   Practical Tips... 92
Chapter eleven...**102**
   Resources and contact... 102
Conclusion..**111**

Chapter one

Introduction

An outline of the Maldives
The Indian Ocean archipelago of the Maldives is a tropical paradise known for its vivid coral reefs, pristine turquoise waters, and stunning natural beauty. This South Asian country, which consists of more than 1,000 coral islands and 26 atolls, is a dream come true for tourists looking

for a peaceful getaway and a peek into an unrivaled world of luxury.

Geography and Location: The Maldives is the smallest country in Asia in terms of both population and land area. It is located southwest of Sri Lanka and India. The islands are scattered across the equator, creating a chain of coral atolls that crosses the Indian Ocean's trading routes.

Major Cities and Capital: Malé, the capital of the Maldives, is a thriving metropolis renowned for its dynamic urban atmosphere, historic sites, and colorful markets. Addu City, Fuvahmulah, and Kulhudhuffushi are a few additional important cities, with Malé serving as the political and economic hub.

Climate: The dry northeast monsoon (Iruvai) from December to March and the rainy southwest monsoon (Hulhangu) from May to October are the two different seasons of the Maldives' tropical climate. The Maldives is a year-round destination with reliably warm temperatures.

Language and Culture: The Maldives' rich historical background is reflected in its culture, which is a fusion of South Asian, Arabian, and African elements. Islam is the prevalent religion, influencing daily life, customs, and holidays. Dhivehi is the official language.

Economy: The Maldives' economy depends heavily on tourism, which also raises the country's GDP. The Maldives has embraced luxury travel, drawing tourists looking for world-class diving and snorkeling, immaculate beaches, and upscale overwater villas.

Amazing Marine Life: The Maldives is well known for having a wide variety of vibrant coral reefs and unusual undersea creatures. The atolls offer a refuge for marine wildlife, which attracts snorkelers and divers.

Preservation Efforts: The Maldives has taken action to save its delicate ecosystems in light of the growing significance of environmental protection. The Maldives' dedication to protecting its natural treasures is demonstrated by its efforts to tackle climate change, promote sustainable tourism, and conserve the marine environment.

A Luxurious Escape: The Maldives provides a variety of lodging options, from lavish overwater villas to quaint beachside resorts, whether it's a romantic retreat, a family holiday, or a single trip. Every island offers a private sanctuary, guaranteeing guests an exceptional and unique experience.

This introduction lays the groundwork for a Maldivian tour, beckoning visitors to experience the allure of this dreamy location and become engrossed in the splendor of its islands and the friendliness of its people.
A succinct overview of culture and history

Overview of History: The Maldives' history is a tapestry made from the influences of many different cultures and civilizations. Over the ages, the archipelago has served as a hub for commercial routes and cross-cultural contacts due to its advantageous location in the Indian Ocean.

Ancient History: The Maldives boasts a rich pre-Islamic past that spans more than two millennia. Archaeological discoveries and historical sources bear witness to the influence of African, Middle Eastern, and South Asian cultures on the islands.

Buddhist Era: The Maldives were a Buddhist kingdom until they converted to Islam in the 12th century. On certain islands, the ruins of Buddhist stupas and monasteries serve as a marker for the era.

Islamic Influence: In the 12th century, Arab traders and travelers introduced Islam to the Maldives, influencing the country's identity and customs. Under Islamic governance, the Maldives emerged as a sultanate.

Colonial Era: Due to the Maldives' advantageous location, several European nations, notably the Portuguese and Dutch, fought for control of the islands. The Maldives were a British protectorate until 1965, when they gained independence. The islands eventually came under British protection in the 19th century.

Modern Independence: On July 26, 1965, the Maldives formally separated from British protection and became a constitutional monarchy. After the country became a republic in 1968, the political climate has changed.

Cultural Heritage: The history, isolation, and Islamic customs of the Maldives have all influenced the country's diverse culture.

Language and Literature: Indo-Aryan languages have an impact on the Maldivian language, Dhivehi. Maldivian literature consists of poetry, folktales passed down through the centuries, and historical epics.

Islamic customs: Islam is very important to Maldivians, as seen by the way it influences holidays, daily activities, and cultural customs. Communities gather around mosques, and Islamic holidays are eagerly celebrated.

Traditional Arts: Woodcarving, lacquerwork, and mat weaving are examples of traditional crafts used to showcase Maldivian craftsmanship. The rich colors of traditional attire and elaborate jewelry are a reflection of Maldivian culture.

Music and Dance: The vibrant embodiment of Maldivian culture is Boduberu, a traditional drumming and singing style. Cultural dances, which are frequently presented at festivals, highlight the grace and rhythm that are fundamental to Maldivian customs.

Modern Influences: The Maldives has welcomed modern influences, especially in the areas of globalization and tourism, while maintaining its rich cultural legacy. Resorts and city centers exhibit a fusion of modern and traditional design elements.

Cultural etiquette: When traveling to the Maldives, it is imperative to honor local traditions. It is welcomed when people dress modestly, especially in public areas and on inhabited islands. It's also crucial to be mindful of Islamic customs to avoid offending anyone, especially during prayer times.

Gaining insight into the Maldives' rich history and culture enriches the vacation experience by enabling guests to recognize the richness and variety that characterize this archipelago nation.

Chapter two

Planning your trip

Ideal time to go

With their tropical environment, the Maldives has a welcoming and friendly atmosphere all year round. However, based on personal interests and activities, some months might be better than others. The ideal seasons to travel to the Maldives are broken down as follows:

Winter Season: December through March

Weather: This time of year is perfect for visiting because it is dry and sunny. There is not much rain, and the pleasant temperatures range from 77°F to 88°F (25°C to 31°C).

Activities: Diving and snorkeling with excellent visibility. Perfect for water activities and beach getaways.

Special activities: Resorts frequently host special activities on New Year's Eve, which is a lively celebration.

Season of Intermonsoon (April to June):

Weather: The change in climate from the dry to the wet season. The weather is still warm, but the amount of rain has somewhat increased.

Activities: It's still appropriate for beach vacations, although there may be sporadic downpours. The circumstances for diving are favorable.

May through October is the Southwest Monsoon.

Weather: More rainfall and more humidity, particularly from June to August. The range of temperatures is 25°C to 31°C (77°F to 88°F).

Activities: Despite the increased frequency of rain, diving is still recommended because there is a wealth of marine life. Certain islands have good surfing conditions.

November, Northeast Monsoon:

Weather: The dry season begins as the southwest monsoon ends. reduction in precipitation and better weather overall.

Activities: As the weather stabilizes, it's good for snorkeling and diving. There may be pre-Christmas events in resorts.

Things to Take Into Account:

Crowds: Due of its popularity during the dry season (December to February in particular), there are usually more tourists and higher rates. The shoulder seasons are a good option if you want a more sedate experience.

Budget: Booking travel during the rainier months can result in lower lodging and activity costs.

Special Events: Think about particular festivals or events you would wish to attend, including neighborhood festivities or activities featuring marine life.

Overall Suggested Action:

It is mostly up to you to decide when would be the best time to visit the Maldives. The dry season is perfect if you want bright, dry weather for beach lounging and water sports. However, the intermonsoon and southwest monsoon seasons can still provide an amazing experience if you're willing to tolerate the odd downpour as well as cheaper costs and less tourists.

prerequisites for visas

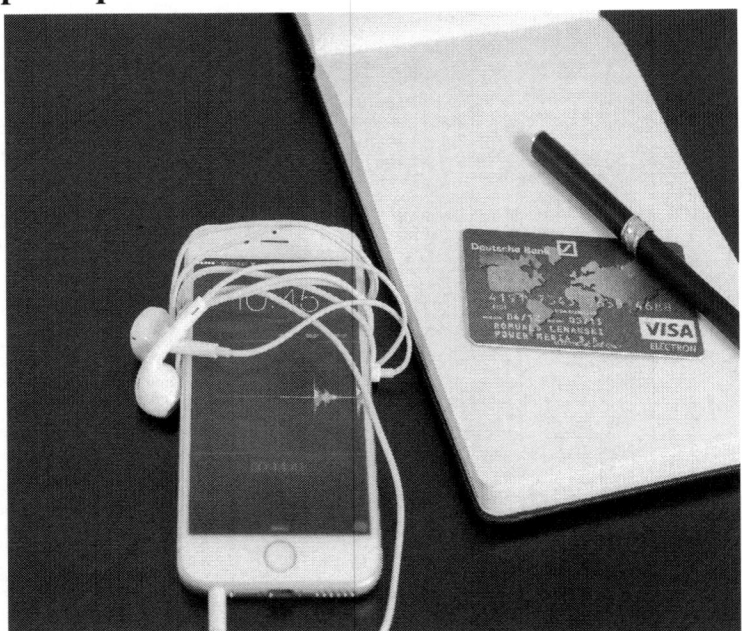

The Maldives' visa requirements are subject to change as of the deadline in January 2022, therefore it's important to confirm the most recent details with government agencies or the Maldivian embassy or consulate in your nation. The majority of travelers' visa requirements are summarized as follows:

Entry Without a Visa:
Tourist Visas: For stays of up to 30 days, the majority of travelers to the Maldives do not need a prearranged visa. This is applicable to citizens of a wide range of nations, including the US, all EU member states, Canada, Australia, and many more.

Visa on Arrival: Upon arrival, if you are eligible for admission without a visa, you will be issued a 30-day visa.

Extension of Visit:
Extensions longer than the first thirty days can be feasible, however you should confirm the particular conditions and steps with Maldives Immigration.

Entry Requirements:
a passport that is currently valid for at least six months after the date of admission.
Evidence of subsequent trip (return ticket).
Enough cash or credit cards to cover your stay costs.
Information about lodging or a hotel reservation.

Work Permit and Extended Stay Visas:
You could require a special visa if you intend to work in the Maldives or stay there for a prolonged length of time. In the Maldives, work permits and long-term visas are usually arranged by the employer or sponsor.

Health Requirements:
Certain health rules can be relevant, especially if you are passing through or coming from an area where certain diseases are endemic. Before you travel, make sure you have any necessary health certificates or immunizations.

Customs Declarations:
Understand the rules governing customs, especially as they relate to the import and export of commodities. Certain things can be prohibited, and you should abide by local laws and cultural customs.

Most recent information

Visa regulations are subject to change, therefore it's important to verify the most recent details on the Maldives Immigration official website or by contacting the Maldivian embassy or consulate in your nation.

To guarantee a simple and hassle-free entry into the Maldives, always make sure you have the most recent information regarding visa requirements before booking your trip. It is the responsibility of travelers to comprehend and abide by the nationality-specific visa requirements.

Tips for budgeting and money

Currency: The Maldivian Rufiyaa (MVR) is the official currency of the Maldives. Nonetheless, most transactions are conducted in US dollars (USD), which is widely recognized and used, particularly in the travel and tourism industry. In resorts and well-known tourist locations, rates are frequently stated in US dollars.

TipsforBudgeting:

Credit cards and cash:

Cash: Although most resorts and cities accept credit cards, it's a good idea to have some local cash (Rufiyaa) on hand for smaller businesses and local markets.

ATMs: A few populated islands, including Malé, have ATMs. It's a good idea to get cash out of an ATM in Malé before visiting isolated islands where they might not be available.

Low-cost Accommodations:

Although the Maldives is most known for its opulent resorts, there are also reasonably priced guesthouses and native island lodging options. It can be less expensive to stay on populated islands than at resorts.

Comprehensive Bundles:

If you intend to stay at a resort, take into account the all-inclusive packages that include entertainment, meals, and even trips. You can better manage your finances by doing this.

Dining Locally:

Discover authentic Maldivian cuisine at more reasonable costs from local cafes on inhabited islands than from resort dining. Try the native cuisine, which includes garudhiya, mas huni, and fish curry from the Maldives.

Transport:

Transporting goods across islands can be expensive. Public ferries are less expensive but could operate on a restricted timetable. Seaplanes and speedboats are more expensive but faster. Consider your time and financial limits while making your transportation plans.

Trips and Events:

To keep costs under control, schedule your outings and hobbies in advance. Package offers or group discounts should be taken into consideration as excursions such as island hopping, snorkeling, and diving can add up.

Purchasing:

Resort souvenir shops could charge more. Look into the local markets in Malé and other inhabited islands for more reasonably priced products. Prices are frequently negotiated at local markets.

Gratuity:

Although not required, leaving a tip is appreciated. A service charge may be added to the bill at certain upscale resorts. It is customary in nearby establishments to round up the bill.

Travelers' Insurance:

Having comprehensive travel insurance is advised to cover unforeseen costs, such as medical crises and missed flights.

Seasonality to Consider:

It could be less expensive to travel during the off-peak season to get lodging and activities. But pay attention to the weather during the monsoon seasons.

Though the Maldives are frequently thought of as a luxury destination, you may still enjoy its splendor on a range of budgets with careful planning. To guarantee a hassle-free and economical travel, it's always a good idea to do your homework and make advance plans.

Chapter three

Getting Around

Options   For   Flights

The Maldives is well-connected by air because it is a well-liked worldwide tourism destination. You can fly to the Maldives using the following choices when you arrange your trip:

Flights Directed:

The primary international airport in the Maldives, Velana International Airport (MLE), is situated close to the capital, Malé, and is served by a number of major airlines. While the number of airlines offering direct flights may vary, non-stop services are frequently offered by airlines from the Middle East, Europe, and Asia.

Flights Connecting:

You can choose connecting flights if there are no direct flights available from your departure point. Major international hubs like Dubai, Doha, Istanbul, Singapore, Bangkok, and Colombo are frequently used as layover locations.

Flights Operating in the Maldives:

Flights to the Maldives are offered by airlines from different areas. As examples, consider:

Middle Eastern airlines: Etihad, Emirates, and Qatar.

Turkish Airlines, Lufthansa, and British Airways serve Europe.

Asia: Singapore Airlines, Cathay Pacific, and Thai Airways. Air India and SriLankan Airlines serve South Asia.

Flights on Charter:

There are travel agencies and tour operators who could provide charter flights to well-known resort locations in the Maldives. These flights might offer a more smooth travel experience, particularly if a certain resort island is your ultimate destination.

Transfers by Seaplane:

You may need to take a domestic flight and then a seaplane transfer if you're going to a resort on a far-off island. One popular way to go to more remote atolls and resorts is via seaplane.

Duration of Flight:

The length of the flight to the Maldives varies based on where you travel from and how many layovers you have. Major hubs can be reached by direct flights in 8 to 12 hours, however longer routes may require connecting flights.

Optimal Reservation Procedures:

Booking your flights far in advance is advised, particularly if you intend to visit during popular times of the year. To evaluate costs and locate the best offers, use internet travel companies or airline websites.

Considering a visa:

Verify the visa requirements for any places you plan to stop over. Make appropriate travel arrangements since certain countries might need transit visas.

Arrival Transportation:

Depending on the resort or island you have selected, getting to your ultimate destination from Velana International Airport may need a domestic flight, speedboat, or seaplane transfer.

Keep in mind that entry rules, visa requirements, and travel restrictions are subject to change, particularly in reaction to international events like the COVID-19 epidemic. It is advisable to verify flight details and other pertinent travel information closer to the day of departure.

Details about the airport

The primary international entry point into the Maldives is Velana International Airport, formerly known as Ibrahim Nasir International Airport. Situated close to Malé, the capital, on Hulhulé Island, the airport is the main point of entry for travelers arriving by air. The following is important information regarding Velana International Airport:

Where:

The Maldives' capital city of Malé is located next to Velana International Airport on Hulhulé Island.

Airport Code:

Velana International Airport has the ICAO code VRMM and the IATA code MLE.

Terminals:

There is a primary passenger terminal at the airport that manages both domestic and international aircraft. It has recently undergone extensive renovations and additions to meet the increasing number of guests.

Services and Facilities:

A variety of amenities and services are available at Velana International Airport, such as duty-free stores, dining options, lounges, currency exchange, ATMs, and a medical center. Passengers with disabilities can also use the amenities.

Transport:

Options for ground transportation consist of public buses, airport shuttles, and taxis. A lot of hotels and resorts provide their visitors transportation services. In addition, the airport serves domestic flights and seaplanes that fly to farther-flung island locations.

Airline:

In addition to housing a number of foreign airlines with flights to and from key cities across the globe, Velana International Airport acts as a hub for the national carrier, Maldivian.

Runways:

There is only one runway at the airport, which is called 18/36 and is around 3,400 meters (11,155 ft) long. A variety of aircraft, including bigger international carriers, can land on the runway.

Visa upon arrival:

The Maldives allows visitors of many nations to obtain a visa upon arrival for stays of up to 30 days. Before departing, make sure to verify the most recent visa requirements specific to your country of citizenship.

COVID-19 Guidelines:

At Velana International Airport, precautions for health and safety have been implemented in response to the continuing global epidemic. In order to guarantee passenger safety, this may involve temperature checks, health declarations, and other procedures.

WiFi:

Passengers can use the free Wi-Fi at the airport. While at the terminal, you can use the airport's network to access the internet.

Desk of Information:

Passengers can get assistance from an information desk at the airport with questions about flights, services, and general information.

It is essential to check the airport website or official sources for up-to-date information on services, amenities, and any advisories regarding travel before departing. Furthermore, keep yourself updated on any entrance restrictions or health precautions that may be in place as a result of the current international crisis.

Chapter four

Accommodations

Options for flights

The Maldives is well-connected by air because it is a well-liked worldwide tourism destination. You can fly to the Maldives using the following choices when you arrange your trip:

Flights Directed:

The primary international airport in the Maldives, Velana International Airport (MLE), is situated close to the capital, Malé, and is served by a number of major airlines. While the number

31

of airlines offering direct flights may vary, non-stop services are frequently offered by airlines from the Middle East, Europe, and Asia.

Flights Connecting:

You can choose connecting flights if there are no direct flights available from your departure point. Major international hubs like Dubai, Doha, Istanbul, Singapore, Bangkok, and Colombo are frequently used as layover locations.

Flights Operating in the Maldives:

Flights to the Maldives are offered by airlines from different areas. As examples, consider:

Middle Eastern airlines: Etihad, Emirates, and Qatar.

Turkish Airlines, Lufthansa, and British Airways serve Europe.

Asia: Singapore Airlines, Thai Airways, and Cathay Pacific.Air India and SriLankan Airlines serve South Asia.

Flights on Charter:

There are travel agencies and tour operators who could provide charter flights to well-known resort locations in the Maldives. These flights might offer a more smooth travel experience, particularly if a certain resort island is your ultimate destination.

Transfers by Seaplane:

You may need to take a domestic flight and then a seaplane transfer if you're going to a resort on a far-off island. One popular way to go to more remote atolls and resorts is via seaplane.

Duration of Flight:

The length of the flight to the Maldives varies based on where you travel from and how many layovers you have. Major hubs can be reached by direct flights in 8 to 12 hours, however longer routes may require connecting flights.

Optimal Reservation Procedures:

Booking your flights far in advance is advised, particularly if you intend to visit during popular times of the year. To evaluate costs and locate the best offers, use internet travel companies or airline websites.

Considering a visa:

Verify the visa requirements for any places you plan to stop over. Make appropriate travel arrangements since certain countries might need transit visas.

Arrival Transportation:

Depending on the resort or island you have selected, getting to your ultimate destination from Velana International Airport may need a domestic flight, speedboat, or seaplane transfer.

Keep in mind that entry rules, visa requirements, and travel restrictions are subject to change, particularly in reaction to international events like the COVID-19 epidemic. It is advisable to verify flight details and other pertinent travel information closer to the day of departure.

Details about the airport

The primary international entry point into the Maldives is Velana International Airport, formerly known as Ibrahim Nasir International Airport. Situated close to Malé, the capital, on Hulhulé Island, the airport is the main point of entry for travelers arriving by air. The following is important information regarding Velana International Airport:

Where:

The Maldives' capital city of Malé is located next to Velana International Airport on Hulhulé Island.

Airport Code:

Velana International Airport has the ICAO code VRMM and the IATA code MLE.

Terminals:

There is a primary passenger terminal at the airport that manages both domestic and international aircraft. It has recently undergone extensive renovations and additions to meet the increasing number of guests.

Services and Facilities:

A variety of amenities and services are available at Velana International Airport, such as duty-free stores, dining options, lounges, currency exchange, ATMs, and a medical center. Passengers with disabilities can also use the amenities.

Transport:

Options for ground transportation consist of public buses, airport shuttles, and taxis. A lot of hotels and resorts provide their visitors transportation services. In addition, the airport serves domestic flights and seaplanes that fly to farther-flung island locations.

Airline:

In addition to housing a number of foreign airlines with flights to and from key cities across the globe, Velana International Airport acts as a hub for the national carrier, Maldivian.

Runways:

There is only one runway at the airport, which is called 18/36 and is around 3,400 meters (11,155 ft) long. A variety of aircraft, including bigger international carriers, can land on the runway.

Visa upon arrival:

The Maldives allows visitors of many nations to obtain a visa upon arrival for stays of up to 30 days. Before departing, make sure to verify the most recent visa requirements specific to your country of citizenship.

COVID-19 Guidelines:

At Velana International Airport, precautions for health and safety have been implemented in response to the continuing global epidemic. In order to guarantee passenger safety, this may involve temperature checks, health declarations, and other procedures.

WiFi:

Passengers can use the free Wi-Fi at the airport. While at the terminal, you can use the airport's network to access the internet.

Desk of Information:

Passengers can get assistance from an information desk at the airport with questions about flights, services, and general information.

It is essential to check the airport website or official sources for up-to-date information on services, amenities, and any advisories regarding travel before departing. Furthermore, keep yourself updated on any entrance restrictions or health precautions that may be in place as a result of the current international crisis.

Chapter five

Activities and Attractions

places for diving and snorkeling

With some of the most amazing underwater scenery, colorful coral reefs, and a wide variety of marine life, the Maldives is a paradise for snorkelers and divers. Here are a few of the best places in the Maldives for

diving and snorkeling:

1. Male Atoll, North:

Diving Locations: Manta Point, HP Reef, and Banana Reef provide gorgeous coral formations, a variety of marine life, and opportunities to see sharks and manta rays.

Snorkeling: The house reef of Lankanfinolhu Island's pristine waters and plethora of marine life make it a great place to go snorkeling.

2. Atoll of South Male:

Diving Sites: Divers can expect to see colorful coral gardens, sharks, and eagle rays at Cocoa Thila, Guraidhoo Corner, and Kandooma Thila.
Snorkeling: Turtles and other marine life can be seen while snorkeling at Biyadhoo Island and Rihiveli Beach.

3. Ari Atoll
Sites for Diving: Maaya Thila, Kudarah Thila, and Fish Head are well-known for their encounters with pelagic animals, such as hammerhead and whale sharks.
Snorkeling: With a variety of fish and coral formations, Dhigurah Island and the reefs around Omadhoo Island provide great snorkeling options.

4. Atoll of Baa:
Scuba Diving Locations: Hanifaru Bay, a UNESCO Biosphere Reserve, is well-known for its clusters of manta rays. Diverse marine life can be found in Dharavandhoo Thila and Dhonfanu Thila.

Snorkeling: Especially in their respective seasons, Baa Atoll is among the best locations to snorkel with whale sharks and manta rays.

5. Atoll of Vaavu:
Sites for Diving: Due to their powerful currents that draw huge pelagic species, Fotteyo Kandu and Alimatha Jetty are well-known for diving. Alimatha Jetty night dives are well known for their chances of seeing nurse sharks.
Snorkeling: The island of Fulidhoo has stunning house reefs with vibrant fish and coral formations that are perfect for snorkeling.

6. Atoll of Lhaviyani:
Dive Sites: Schools of fish, rays, and sharks can all be found in the diverse marine life of Okobe Thila, Fushivaru Thila, and Kuredu Express.
Snorkeling: Kuredu Island's house reef provides fantastic snorkeling opportunities, with the possibility of seeing reef sharks and turtles.

7. Atoll of Laamu:

Scuba Diving Locations: Hithadhoo Corner and Gan Kandu are well-known for their powerful currents and opportunities to see sharks and rays.
Snorkeling: You may experience the underwater beauty through snorkeling tours around the atoll and the house reef at Six Senses Laamu.

8. Addu Atoll:
Sites for Diving: British Loyalty Wreck and Koattey Beyru provide distinctive diving opportunities, including the opportunity to examine a sunken British cruiser.
Snorkeling: With a diverse range of marine life, the atoll's waterways and coral formations offer great snorkeling opportunities.

9. Meemu Atoll:
Sites for Diving: Reef sharks and manta rays are among the many species of marine life that can be found at Manta Point and Vattaru Kandu.
Snorkeling: Take pleasure in snorkeling Muli Island and the atoll's waterways to explore its underwater treasures.

10. Thaa Atoll: - Diving Sites: Known for their colorful coral gardens, varied marine life, and sporadic shark sightings, Munnafushi Kandu and Veymandoo Kandu are popular diving spots.

- Snorkeling: With their vibrant corals and fish, Thimarafushi Island and the nearby reefs make for excellent snorkeling spots.

These are but a handful of the numerous dive and snorkel spots available throughout the atolls of the Maldives. Remember that seasonal variations can affect the finest spots, so it's best to check with local dive centers for the most recent details and suggestions.

Water activities

For those seeking excitement, the Maldives has a variety of thrilling water activities in its turquoise, crystal-clear waters. There is something for everyone, whether your preference is for the peace and quiet of studying marine life or the adrenaline of high-speed adventures. In the Maldives, the following water activities are very popular:

**1. Scuba Diving:

Snorkeling is a great way to see the colorful coral reefs and aquatic creatures. House reefs are easily accessible from many resorts, and guided snorkeling trips are also offered.

**2. Underwater Photography:
A popular place for scuba diving worldwide is the Maldives. Discover stunning coral gardens and underwater caverns. You may also come across a variety of marine life, like as colorful fish, rays, and sharks.

**3. Having a surf session:
Due to its world-class surf breaks, the Maldives is a popular destination for surfers. Surfing packages are available from resorts in the Atolls, and several islands provide reliable waves that are good for surfers of all abilities.

**4. The art of windsurfing:
The Maldives is a great place to windsurf because of its tranquil lagoons and consistent trade winds. Equipment rental and windsurfing lessons are available at many resorts.

**5. Inflatable kayaking:

The Maldives offers great winds and open oceans for kiteboarding enthusiasts. Beginners can take advantage of the available lessons, and experienced kiteboarders can make the most of the excellent conditions.

**6. SUP, or stand-up paddleboarding:

A well-liked and soothing method of exploring the tranquil waters surrounding the islands is via paddleboarding. Resorts frequently have SUP boards for hire.

**7. Water skiing:

In the crystal-clear waters of the Maldives, enjoy the exhilaration of jet skiing. For those looking for an adrenaline thrill, many resorts rent out jet skis and provide guided trips.

**8. Sailing a parasol:

Parasail above the lagoons and take in the breath-taking panoramas of the atolls. Many water sports facilities and resorts provide this activity.

**9. Canoeing:

Kayak through the mangroves and shallow lagoons. Most facilities have kayaks accessible, which offer a tranquil opportunity to take in the breathtaking scenery.

**10. Sailing Catamarans: - Sail a catamaran at a leisurely pace and take in the tranquility of the Maldivian waters. Sailing courses and catamaran trips are provided by certain resorts.

**11. Fishing: - Try your hand at deep-sea fishing or use the customary methods used in the Maldives. Fishing trips are frequently organized by resorts; you might catch game fish like barracuda or tuna.

Underwater Scooter

**12. Take a spin on an underwater scooter for a novel experience. With the help of these scooters, you can easily explore the underwater environment.

The underwater scooter known as a "seabob" enables one to effortlessly maneuver around the water. They provide an exciting and enjoyable approach to discover the underwater environment.

The Maldives has a range of water sports to fit your tastes, whether you're an adrenaline junkie or you want a slower pace. For all skill levels, equipment rental, instruction, and guided excursions are offered by resorts and water sports centers.

Cultural encounters

The Maldives have a rich cultural past that is just waiting to be discovered, despite being well-known for its breathtaking natural beauty and opulent resorts. You can partake in the following cultural activities when visiting the Maldives:

**1. Travel to Malé

Discover the Maldivian way of life by touring the nation's capital, Malé. See the Old Friday Mosque (Hukuru Miskiy), the Malé Fish Market, and the Maldives Islamic Centre.

**2. Day Trips to Local Islands:

Visit inhabited nearby islands on day trips or guided tours to meet the amiable inhabitants, discover their traditional crafts, and take in each island's distinct culture.

3. Take in a Performance of Bodu Beru:
Rhythmic chanting and drumming define the traditional Maldivian music and dance performance known as Bodu Beru. Go see a Bodu Beru performance to see this vibrant display of culture.

4. Food from the Maldives:
Savor Maldivian food to get a taste of the islands' flavors. Sample some of the regional specialties, like garudhiya (fish soup), fihunu mas (grilled fish), and mas huni (tuna and coconut salad).

5. Regional Crafts and Arts:
Look for beautiful lacquerware, woven mats, and wooden dhonis (traditional Maldivian boats) among the traditional handicrafts available at the local markets and shops.

6. Customary Dance of the Maldives:
Take in traditional dance performances from the Maldives, such the Thaara dance, which are frequently held during festivals and cultural events.

7. Islamic Center of Maldives:

Explore the architectural wonder that is the Maldives Islamic Centre in Malé, renowned for its imposing golden dome. Find out about the cultural customs and Islamic legacy of the nation.

**8. Festivals of Culture:

Consider scheduling your trip to coincide with one of the Maldives' cultural celebrations, such Maldives Independence Day or Eid al-Fitr. These gatherings feature regional customs, music, and dancing.

**9. Conventional Clothes, Dhivehi Libaas: - Try on Dhivehi libaas, the traditional Maldivian attire, which consists of a vibrant dress for women and a sarong-like item for men called a mundu. Certain resorts provide opportunities for cultural clothing.

**10. Traditional Maldivian Medicine: - Find out about the generations-old use of indigenous herbs and treatments in traditional Maldivian medicine. Certain resorts might provide wellness programs based on conventional wisdom.

**11. Thundi, the Customary Swing: - Learn how to do the Thundi, a traditional Maldivian swing that is frequently performed in the area. It's a straightforward but entertaining aspect of Maldivian culture, particularly on celebratory days.

**12. Take Part in Local Events: - Take part in the celebrations and festivals if your visit falls during one of the local occasions. The people of the Maldives are kind, and taking part in cultural activities helps one get a greater understanding of the local customs.

**13. Explore Local Mosques: Observe the distinctive architecture and take in religious practices by visiting local mosques situated on inhabited islands. Keep in mind to cover up when visiting places of worship.

Your understanding of the local way of life and the cultural diversity that accentuates the islands' natural beauty will grow as a result of include these cultural events in your Maldives itinerary.

Chapter six

Local Cuisine

Customary cuisine from the Maldives

The cuisine of the Maldives is a delicious fusion of flavors influenced by the Middle East, Sri Lanka, and the Indian subcontinent. The abundance of marine resources in the Maldives is reflected in the important role that seafood plays in local meals. You should sample the following typical Maldivian cuisine:

**1. Huni Mas:

Mas huni, a well-liked breakfast meal in the Maldives, consists of tuna, coconut, onion, chili, and lime. Usually, it is eaten with roshi or flatbread.

**2. The Garudhiya:

Traditional fish soup garudhiya is prepared using tuna, coconut milk, lime, chili, and onion. It's typically served with rice noodles, flatbread, or both.

**3. The Grilled Fish, or Fihunu Mas:

The Maldivians have a reputation for being skilled fish grillers. A mixture of Maldivian spices is used to marinate tuna or other local fish, which is then expertly grilled to perfection, to make fihunu mas.

**4. Roshi:

A common dish in the cuisine of the Maldives is rozhi. Usually, it's served with a dollop of coconut and tuna, mas huni, or one of several curries.

**5. Keemiya Bis:

Bis keemiya, an Indian pastry filled with fish, coconut, and spices, is similar to a samosa. It is deep-fried. It's a widely consumed snack in the Maldives.

**6. Mas Huni Fihunu:

This dish makes a tasty and filling supper by combining grilled fish (fihunu mas) with mas huni. It's frequently served with roshi or rice.

**7. Hiti Bambukeylu:

A meal called bambukeylu hiti is prepared with grated coconut, chili, and breadfruit. The meal is made savory and spicy by combining and cooking the components.

Boshi Mashuni: **8

A blend of finely shredded banana blossom, coconut, onion, chile, and lime is called boshi mashuni salad. It's a wholesome and revitalizing dish.

**9. Masroshi: - A variety of stuffed flatbread containing a blend of fish, coconut, onion, and spices is called masroshi. It's deep-fried or baked to a rich brown.

**10. Curry chicken, or Kukulhu Riha: - The Maldives is known for its fish, but chicken curry is also a staple meal. Coconut milk and a mixture of regional spices are used to make the curry.

11. Kiru Sarbat: An energizing beverage prepared from the toddy palm tree's essence is called kiru sarbat. It tastes sweet and is savored as a beverage in the summer.

12. Dhivehi Riha, or Maldivian Curry: The name "dhivehi riha" refers to a variety of Maldivian curries, such as beef, chicken, or fish curry. The curry is seasoned with coconut milk and a blend of regional spices.

13. Spicy Tuna, Kulhimas: - A spicy tuna dish called kulhimas is made using shredded tuna, coconut, chili, and other seasonings. It's frequently served with flatbread or rice.

Savor these traditional meals when dining in the Maldives; don't pass them up. Maldivian cuisine is available at many resorts and neighborhood restaurants, giving visitors a genuine flavor of the nation's gastronomic legacy.

Options for dining

Traditional Maldivian food and foreign cuisine are only two of the many eating options available in the Maldives to suit a wide range of palates. You can try the following various dining establishments in the Maldives:

**1. Dining establishments at resorts:
The majority of Maldivian resorts feature several on-site eateries serving a variety of dishes, such as Maldivian, Asian, European, and more. These eateries frequently provide varied breakfast, lunch, and supper menus.

**2. Dining by the Water:
Savor the distinct excitement of dining above the river. Many resorts have dining pavilions or overwater restaurants where you can indulge in delicious meals while taking in breath-blowing views of the ocean.

**3. Restaurants Beneath the Sea:
Underwater restaurants at select opulent Maldivian resorts offer a fantastic dining experience amidst marine life. These eateries frequently offer fine dining in a very distinctive atmosphere.

**4. Dining by the Beach:

Savor the beautiful atmosphere of dining by the beach. A lot of resorts have private beach dinners where you may enjoy mouthwatering meals beneath the stars while sitting with your feet on the sand.

**5. Food and Wine Cruises:

Take a dinner cruise by day or by night. Certain resorts provide exclusive boat excursions that include fine dining served while cruising the Maldivian waterways.

**6. Tea Houses in Maldives:

Experience the traditional food and drinks of the Maldives by visiting local tea houses on inhabited islands. Savor regional specialties like Mas Huni, sweet desserts, and quick bites.

**7. Grills on the Island:

Numerous resorts provide island barbecues where you may indulge in grilled meats, fish, and fresh salads in a relaxed atmosphere.

**8. Design-Based Dining:

A "Dining by Design" idea is available at certain resorts, enabling visitors to personalize their eating experience. Pick a private space, decide on your menu, and savor a customized dinner in an elegant atmosphere.

Restaurants in the Area on Inhabited Islands: Visit nearby islands to discover authentic Maldivian restaurants. These places provide an opportunity to sample traditional Maldivian cuisine and discover regional delicacies.

**10. Themed Nights: Resorts frequently have themed evenings when guests can savor a buffet with international cuisine. Live performances by artists and entertainers could be a part of these events.

**11. Maldivian Cooking lessons: Under the direction of experienced chefs, you can learn how to prepare traditional cuisine at some resorts that offer Maldivian cooking lessons.

**12. In-Villa Dining: Several resorts include in-villa dining options so you can eat fine dining in the comfort of your own lodging if you prefer seclusion.

**13. calm Cafés and Bars: Resorts usually feature calm cafés and bars where you may enjoy light fare, coffee, and tropical drinks in a laid-back setting.

The Maldives offers a range of options to fit your interests, whether you're looking for an adventurous dining experience, a simple seaside lunch, or a romantic supper. It's a good idea to check out the resort's dining options and ask about any special dining events they might have during your visit.

Chapter seven

Health and safety

Insurance for travel

vacation insurance is a crucial component of trip planning, offering financial security and piece of mind in case unexpected circumstances disrupt or influence your vacation plans. Here are some important things to consider when thinking about getting travel insurance for your trip to the Maldives:

**1. Protection Against Trip Abrupture or Cancellation:
Make sure your travel insurance covers interruptions or cancellations brought on by unanticipated circumstances like emergency, illness, or injury. Coverage for non-refundable costs like travel and lodging may fall under this category.
**2. Health Insurance:
Make sure the complete medical coverage provided by your travel insurance covers costs

for any illnesses or injuries that may arise while you are traveling. Repatriation and medical evacuation should be covered.

**3. Insurance Against Missed Connections or Travel Delays:
Seek coverage that pays you back for extra costs if your itinerary is disrupted by unanticipated events, missing connections, or delays in your travels.

**4. Misplaced or Theft Property:
Make sure that your insurance covers misplaced, stolen, or destroyed property, such as personal effects, luggage, and critical records.

**5. Services for Emergency Assistance:
Verify whether you have 24/7 emergency assistance coverage with your travel insurance. This can be quite helpful if you need assistance locating hospitals, planning an escape, or handling other problems.

**6. Travel Warnings and Natural Disasters:
Certain travel insurance plans offer protection in the event of natural disasters or travel advisories that could interfere with your intended itinerary.

Check the terms and conditions pertaining to these circumstances.

7. Coverage of Adventure Activities:

Make sure your insurance covers water sports and other adventurous activities if you intend to partake in them while visiting the Maldives. Certain high-risk behaviors may be prohibited by some standard policies.

8. Pre-existing Health Issues:

When getting travel insurance, be sure to disclose any pre-existing medical issues. Pre-existing condition clauses may be specifically mentioned in some policies, and coverage may differ.

9. Length of Coverage: - Verify that the coverage lasts for the whole length of your trip, including any post- or pre-trip extensions.

10. Examine Policy Exclusions: Read the policy exclusions carefully to see which circumstances or occurrences could not be covered. Exclusions that are frequently cited include dangerous activities, travel to high-risk locations, and several forms of extreme sports.

11. Verify Your COVID-19 Insurance:

- In light of the current international circumstances, confirm if COVID-19-related concerns, such as trip cancellations, medical costs, or quarantine costs, are covered by your travel insurance.

**12. Insurance Provider Reputation: Pick a trustworthy insurance company that has a history of prompt claim processing and excellent customer service. Examine evaluations and take into account suggestions from other visitors.

Read the terms and conditions of the policy carefully, paying attention to any fine print, before acquiring travel insurance. Please don't hesitate to contact the insurance company if you have any specific queries or worries. Purchasing travel insurance is an investment in your financial security and peace of mind when traveling.

Safety measures for health
It's crucial to take health measures before visiting the Maldives in order to guarantee a fun

and safe vacation. Consider the following health advice and safety measures:

**1. Immunizations:
Make sure all of your recommended immunizations are current. You could require immunizations against influenza, typhoid, and hepatitis A and B, depending on your travel history and unique circumstances. For tailored advice, consult your healthcare practitioner.

**2. Guidelines for COVID-19:
Keep up with the most recent COVID-19 recommendations and Maldivian entrance requirements. This contains details about immunization schedules, testing, and quarantine procedures. Pay attention to developments from the Maldivian government and health agencies.

**3. Insurance for Travel:
As previously said, think about getting comprehensive travel insurance that covers unanticipated circumstances like medical emergencies and trip cancellations. Make sure that COVID-19-related concerns are covered by the insurance.

**4. Food and Water Safety:

To prevent contracting a waterborne illness, use treated or bottled water. Use caution when consuming seafood that is raw or undercooked and food that is sold by street sellers. Limit your diet to clean, well-cooked foods.

**5. Protection Against Mosquitoes:

Because of the tropical climate in the Maldives, mosquitoes might be common. Apply insect repellent, dress in long sleeves, and think about booking lodging with screened windows to reduce the chance of contracting infections from mosquitoes.

**6. Sunscreen:

Because of the intense sunlight in the Maldives, it's critical to take precautions against sunburn. Wear a hat, use high-SPF sunscreen, and drink plenty of water. When the sun is at its strongest, look for shade to prevent overexposure.

**7. Motion Vertigo:

Be ready for possible motion sickness if you intend to use a boat or seaplane between islands. If you are prone to motion sickness, think about using wristbands or medicine as preventive measures.

**8. Water Sports and Swimming:

When engaging in activities near water, exercise caution. For diving, snorkeling, and other water sports, abide by the safety regulations. If your swimming isn't very good, think about using a life jacket.

**9. Healthcare Facilities: - Though there are medical services in the Maldives, they might not be as plentiful on isolated islands. Staying on islands with better healthcare facilities is something you should think about if you have special medical needs. Always keep a little first aid kit on you.

**10. Local Health Customs: - Learn about the customs and practices related to local health. For instance, when you visit local villages and places of worship, it is polite to cover your knees and shoulders.

**11. Jet lag and motion: To reduce the symptoms of jet lag, make sure you drink plenty of water, get adequate sleep, and think about rearranging your sleep routine before you travel.

Select seats on boats or airplanes that are less likely to cause motion sickness if you are prone to it.

**12. Prescription Drugs: - Make sure you carry enough of your prescribed drugs with you for the duration of your trip. Keep a copy of your prescriptions with you at all times, and be informed of any limitations on importing drugs into the nation.

For tailored health advice and suggestions based on your unique health state and travel plans, speak with your healthcare professional prior to your trip to the Maldives. Remember that health precautions can change, so it's critical to stay up to date on the most recent findings and advice.

Chapter eighth

Shopping and souvenirs

popular goods to purchase
A variety of distinctive, regionally produced goods from the Maldives are available and would make wonderful presents or mementos. Here are a few well-liked products to purchase in the Maldives:

**1. Feyli, or handwoven mats:

Traditional Maldivian feylis are mats composed of natural fibers, usually the leaves of the coconut palm. They are available in a variety of sizes and patterns and are finely woven.

**2. Glass with lacquer:

Maldivian lacquerware is characterized by elaborate decorations on wooden objects including trays, ornaments, and boxes. The procedure is a traditional technique that calls for layers of lacquer.

Crafts Made from Coconut Shells:

Coconut shells are used by artisans to make a variety of products, such as decorative pieces, bowls, and spoons. These products highlight how versatile coconut materials can be.

**4. Indigenous Fabrics (Feyli Libaas):

Handwoven cotton clothes are a staple of Feyli Libaas, the traditional attire of the Maldives. Look for women's gowns, sarongs, and other traditional clothing.

**5. Maldivian mat weaving, or Thundu Kunaa:

Traditionally, mats with exquisite weavings called Thundu Kunaa were used for seating.

They come in a variety of sizes and patterns and are frequently constructed from natural fibers.

**6. Tuna from the Maldives:

The Maldives is renowned for its superior tuna. Tuna goods manufactured locally are available for purchase, such as dried fish, smoked tuna, and canned tuna.

**7. Dhonis, or little boats:

Miniature versions of the dhonis, the native boats of the Maldives, are artistic and unusual keepsakes. They come in different sizes and are frequently carved from wood.

Maldivian jewelry

**8:Seek out traditional jewelry made in the Maldives from materials such as shells and coral. Earrings with elaborate designs, bracelets, and necklaces are possible pieces.

**9. Native Spices: Recreate the tastes of the Maldives at home with spices that are grown nearby. Curry mixes, fish masala, and chilli are examples of Maldivian spices that can give your food a taste of the islands.

**10. Maldivian Souvenir T-Shirts: A lot of gift shops sell T-shirts with traditional Maldivian motifs, marine life, and island-inspired artwork on them.

**11. Maldivian Perfume Oils: - Fragrance connoisseurs may find pleasure in Maldivian perfume oils, which are frequently crafted using indigenous materials and influenced by the islands' tropical aromas.

**12. Local Artwork: Acquire sculptures, paintings, or prints made by regional artists. The vivid marine life, scenery, and cultural facets of the Maldives are frequently depicted in artwork.

**13. Coral crafts and seashell crafts: - Popular mementos are handcrafted objects fashioned from coral and seashells. This can apply to ornaments, jewelry, and other decorative items.

**14. Maldives Handicrafts: - Take a look at the range of handicrafts created by regional artists, including wooden carvings, woven baskets, and traditional Maldivian items.

To locate a wide variety of genuine and handcrafted goods, it's a good idea to browse local markets, artisan stores, and resort boutiques while shopping in the Maldives. Be aware of any export limitations on specific goods, like coral, and practice ethical and sustainable shopping.

regional marketplaces

A wonderful opportunity to fully immerse yourself in Maldivian culture and daily life is to explore local markets. Popular local markets that you can visit are as follows:

**1. The Malé Local Market:
The primary market in the nation's capital is the Malé Local Market, sometimes referred to as the Malé Bazaar or the Malé Fish Market. With booths offering fresh fruit, regional foods, spices, trinkets, and, of course, an abundance of seafood, it has a lively environment.

**2. Malé Fishermen's Market:
The fisherman's Market, which is next to the Malé Local Market, is a busy spot where you can see local fisherman bringing in the day's catch. This is an excellent chance to view a range of fish and seafood, including the well-known tuna from the Maldives.

**3. Island Marketplaces on Different Islands:
There are local markets on several inhabited islands where you can get a more genuine, relaxed vibe. Fresh food, crafts, and locally made goods are frequently available at these markets.

**4. The Island Market at Thulusdhoo (Thulusdhoo):
Discover handmade souvenirs, local foods, and other things at Thulusdhoo's local market. The town is well-known for its surf breaks and traditional crafts.

**5. The Maafushi Island Market:
There are guesthouses on the nearby island of Maafushi, and there's a market there where you can buy local goods and refreshments and socialize with the kind islanders.

**6. Central Park Market in Hulhumalé (Hulhumalé):
Near Central Park on the artificial island of Hulhumalé, near Malé, is a market. Snacks, locally produced goods, and fresh produce are available here.

**7. Market Island at Gulhi (Gulhi):

In addition to having a local market where you may browse handcrafted goods, textiles, and everyday products, Gulhi is well-known for its traditional boatbuilding.

**8. Fish Market in Kulhudhuffushi (Kulhudhuffushi):

In the vibrant fish market of Kulhudhuffushi, in the northern Maldives, you may observe the day-to-day activity of the local fisherman and discover the assortment of seafood available.

**9. Island Market at Ukulhas, Ukulhas:

- Fresh fruit, handcrafted goods, and environmentally friendly products may be found in Ukulhas' local market, which is well-known for its dedication to environmental sustainability.

**10. Thinadhoo Market (Thinadhoo): - Located in the Gaafu Dhaalu Atoll, Thinadhoo features a local market where you may buy locally created goods and observe the daily lives of the locals.

**11. Thaa Atoll Market (Various Islands in Thaa Atoll): Take a look at the local marketplaces on the various islands in Thaa Atoll to get a sense of the distinctive customs and goods that exist there.

It's a good idea to observe local customs and bargaining techniques when visiting local markets. Compared to resort boutiques, these markets provide a more immersive experience by allowing visitors to mingle with locals, sample regional cuisine, and buy handmade trinkets.

Chapter nine

Nightlife and Entertainment

Nightclubs and bars

Although the Maldives are renowned for their peaceful atmosphere, it's vital to remember that the nation adheres to Islamic law, which limits the sale and drinking of alcohol to resorts and liveaboard boats that serve tourists. There are a few authorized locations in the capital city of Malé where visitors can partake in alcoholic beverages. Here are a few choices:

**1. The city of Malé

The Sea House:

In Malé, there's a well-known restaurant and cafe called The Sea House. There is a rooftop space with stunning city and ocean views for guests to take in. The establishment offers both alcoholic and non-alcoholic drink selections.

Shelled Beans:

Another café in Malé that offers tea, coffee, and a variety of non-alcoholic drinks is called Shell Beans. It's a comfortable place to unwind and sip a drink.2. Bars at Resorts:

The majority of Maldivian resorts provide bars where visitors may unwind and take in the scenery while sipping alcoholic beverages. These establishments frequently have overwater or beachside settings with breathtaking views of the nearby lagoons.

**3. Live-aboard Watercraft:

After a day of exploring, visitors can mingle and enjoy beverages in the bars on board several liveaboard vessels that provide diving and cruise experiences in the Maldives.

**4. Malé's Underground Nightclub:

Malé's Underground is a nightclub that periodically holds events and offers a place to mingle and dance. Remember that the nightlife scene is constrained by the cultural setting and laws.

It's critical to abide by local alcohol drinking regulations and norms. Alcohol is not widely available on local islands, and guests are expected to follow Maldivian cultural customs. As the Maldives is mainly recognized for its serene and natural surroundings, other locations in the area could be more appropriate if you're searching for a vibrant nightlife scene with bars and nightclubs. During your stay, make sure you are aware of and abide by all applicable rules and regulations.

artistic presentations

Cultural performances in the Maldives offer an enthralling window into the customs, music, and dance of the surrounding communities. You might see the following kinds of cultural performances while you're there:

Bodu Beru

**1. Traditional Maldivian music and dance known as "Bodu Beru" is distinguished by chanting, intense gestures, and rhythmic drumming. It is frequently performed during festivals, celebrations, and other cultural gatherings.

**2. The Thaara Dancing

The traditional Maldivian dance known as thaara dance features deft footwork and hand gestures. Dancers perform to the rhythm of traditional music while frequently donning vibrant costumes.

**3. Race Events for Dhoni:

Popular cultural events called "dhoni races" feature amicable racing between traditional Maldivian boats, or "dhonis." These occasions honor the local culture in addition to showcasing maritime prowess.

**4. Resort Cultural Shows:

Numerous resorts host cultural events that include storytelling, traditional dance, and music. During these shows, visitors can get a taste of Maldivian culture in a resort environment.

**5. Performances in Boduberu:

Drummers and vocalists make up boduberu troupes, who play exuberant music and traditional dances. These performances frequently use their enthralling rhythms to tell tales and discuss historical occurrences.

**6. Nights of Culture:

Special cultural nights are held by several resorts where visitors can take part in local customs, enjoy traditional music and dance performances, and sample Maldivian cuisine.

**7. Eid festivities:

You might see unique cultural events and performances, such as traditional music and dance, as part of the celebrations on Islamic holidays like Eid al-Fitr.

**8. Festivals of Culture:

In the event that your trip falls during a cultural festival, you should anticipate seeing a range of shows, parades, and customs. Festivals offer a singular chance to fully engage with the culture of the area.

9. small Island Events: During holidays, celebrations, or festivals, you can come across community gatherings with live cultural performances on inhabited small islands.

10. Customary Drumming Rituals: - Ceremonies using traditional drumming are frequently arranged to commemorate important occasions. In these events, the drums' rhythmic beats are very important.

11. Bodu Mas Performances: Bodu Mas is a traditional dance style in which dancers don ornate masks and costumes. The dance is a component of Maldivian cultural heritage and frequently tells stories from mythology.

12. Religious festivities: The Maldives' Islamic customs are reflected in the cultural shows, processions, and unique ceremonies that take place during religious events and festivities.

Inquire about scheduled shows and events during your visit with your resort, the local government on the island, or the event organizers to witness these cultural performances. A great way to enjoy the

Maldives' rich artistic expressions and traditions is through cultural performances.

Chapter ten

Practical Tips

Packing advice

When packing for a trip to the Maldives, take into account the island's tropical weather, beach-focused activities, and any resort- or culture-specific requirements. To help you get ready for your trip to the Maldives, consider the following packing advice:

**1. Airy and Ventilated Apparel:

Bring clothes that is breathable and light enough for the tropical weather. Excellent options include moisture-wicking materials, cotton, and linen. Add T-shirts, shorts, swimwear, and casual beachwear.

**2. Essentials of Sun Protection:

Bring the following items for sun protection because of the intense sunlight:

SPF-rated sunscreen

UV-blocking sunglasses

broad-brimmed cap or hat

Long sleeves and light weight apparel for increased sun protection3. Water-Resistant Equipment:

If you want to do any aquatic sports, think about packing waterproof equipment like a dry bag or waterproof phone case. This will guarantee that your electronics stay dry and protect your possessions from splashes.

**4. Footwear

Bring along cozy flip-flops or sandals for beach excursions. Water shoes with strong traction can be helpful if you intend to snorkel or participate in other water sports. A good pair of walking shoes may be useful for any inland exploration or outings.

**5. First Aid Kit and Medication:

Bring a basic first aid kit and any prescription medications that may be required. Add supplies such as adhesive bandages, pain killers, antihistamines, and other personal prescriptions you may require.

**6. Repellent for Mozzies:

Even while a lot of resorts have mosquito control methods in place, it's still a good idea to pack insect repellent for evenings or if you intend to explore nearby islands.

**7. Equipment for Snorkeling:

While some resorts provide snorkeling equipment, for a more comfortable and customized experience, think about bringing your own. Fins, a mask, and a snorkel can help you explore the colorful underwater environment more fully.

**8. Lightweight Raincoat:

Even if it doesn't rain much, it's still a good idea to bring a lightweight raincoat or poncho in case it does.

9. Devices and Power Sources: - Bring any required electronic equipment, including chargers, smartphones, and cameras. If you intend to use your phone near water, think about getting a waterproof case.

10. Power Adapter: Make sure your electrical devices are powered appropriately by researching the Maldives' power socket types.

11. Travel Documents: - Make sure you have all the paperwork you'll need, such as your passport, airline tickets, hotel bookings, and any applicable visas. Important documents should be photocopied and stored separately.

12. Reusable Water Bottle: - Carry a reusable water bottle to stay hydrated. Reusable bottles can be given by certain resorts, and tap water in the Maldives is usually safe to consume.

13. Cultural Considerations: - If you intend to tour the nearby islands, dress modestly when visiting local villages and religious places. This includes wearing knee- and shoulder-covering apparel.

14. Cash and Credit Cards: - Although credit cards are commonly accepted at resorts, it can be helpful to have some local money, or Maldivian Rufiyaa, on hand for purchases made in Malé or on other islands.

15. Travel Locks: - To protect your items in your lodging and while traveling, use travel locks on your bags.

16. Daypack or Beach Bag: - When touring or lounging at the beach, carry a compact daypack or beach bag with you to hold necessities.

Don't forget to adjust your packing list according to the particular activities you want to partake in and the amenities your resort of choice offers. Furthermore, prior to your journey, make sure you are aware of the most recent travel advisories and standards.

Language and communication

The majority of people in the Maldives speak Dhivehi, which is the official language of the country. English is also commonly used, particularly in the tourism sector, and most Maldivians who work in the hotel industry probably speak the language well. The following are important details regarding language and communication in the Maldives:

**1. Language of Dhivehi:
The native tongue of the Maldivians is Dhivehi, an Indo-Aryan language. For a brief stay, you might not need to study Dhivehi, but the people there will appreciate your effort if you can pick up and use some simple phrases.

**2. Language of English:
In the Maldives, English is extensively spoken, especially in the travel and tourism sector. The majority of tour guides, hotel employees, and others in service and hospitality-related fields are fluent in English. In most tourist destinations, you should be able to interact in English fluently.

**3. Honor regional traditions:
Even though English is widely spoken, particularly in resorts and tourist destinations,

picking up a few simple Dhivehi phrases can show appreciation for the indigenous way of life. Your efforts to converse in their language can be appreciated by the locals.

**4. Interaction on nearby islands:

Although there might be fewer English speakers on inhabited local islands, you can still converse in basic English. Acquiring a few Dhivehi salutations and expressions can improve your communication with the locals.

**5. Communication at the Resort:

The personnel at resorts is used to interacting with visitors from other countries. All official communication, including menus, signage, and events, is primarily conducted in English.

**6. Internet and mobile services:

In the Maldives, mobile and internet services are readily accessible. The majority of visitors can simply maintain connectivity by utilizing international roaming services or local SIM cards.

**7. Guides for Tours:

If you take part in tours or excursions with guides, the guides will probably speak English well and will provide you information about the sights and activities in that language.

**8. Numbers and Currency:

The national currency is the Maldivian Rufiyaa (MVR). Even though prices are frequently shown in both Rufiyaa and US dollars, it's a good idea to become familiar with Dhivehi's basic numerals and local currency.

**9. Help for Emergencies:

English-speaking resort workers or locals who speak the language can help you in an emergency. 119 is the emergency hotline number for law enforcement, firefighters, or ambulance services.Cultural Sensitivity Number Ten: Understanding and showing respect for regional traditions and customs is essential to good communication. In general, Maldivians are amiable and grateful to outsiders who express an interest in their way of life.

In general, English speakers will find it easy to travel the Maldives and communicate with others. Acquiring a few Dhivehi phrases can improve your relationships with the locals and your cultural experience, particularly when it comes to greetings.

Chapter eleven

Resources and contact

Information about emergencies

It's crucial to know the appropriate contact details and protocols in case of an emergency in the Maldives. Here is vital traveler emergency information:

**1. Emergency Services:
* Dial 119 for the emergency hotline in case of fire, medical, or police situations.2. Reaching Out to Your Consulate or Embassy:

Be aware of the phone number and email address of your Maldivian embassy or consulate. Get in touch with the diplomatic mission of your nation if you need assistance with matters pertaining to your nationality or in the event of a significant emergency.

**3. Emergencies in Medicine:
Get in touch with the nearby hospital or healthcare center if you want medical assistance. Additionally, some resorts feature medical facilities, and the personnel can help make medical arrangements.

**4. Dispersed Healthcare Facilities:
Medical facilities in the Maldives are dispersed among several nearby islands. If you are on a populated island, find out where the closest medical facility is.

**5. Services for Evacuations:

Evacuation assistance might be required in the case of a serious medical emergency. Certain resorts offer medical evacuation services via seaplane or boat to Malé, the capital, which has more comprehensive medical facilities.

**6. Services for Search and Rescue:
The Maldives National Defense Force is in charge of maritime search and rescue operations if you are participating in water activities and need search and rescue assistance. For assistance, get in touch with the emergency hotline or the local authorities.

Natural Disasters: **7.
Storms and tsunamis are among the natural disasters that could affect the Maldives. Get acquainted with the escape routes and protocols that your lodging provides. If a tsunami warning is issued, get to higher ground right away.

**8. Consular Support:
Get in touch with your embassy or consulate if you misplace your passport or run into any other problems that call for diplomatic assistance.

They can offer direction on what needs to be done.

**9. Local Governments: If you need help or information in a non-emergency, you can get in touch with the local government or the front desk of your lodging.

**10. Travel Insurance: - Make sure you have all-inclusive travel insurance that addresses unanticipated circumstances like medical emergency and evacuation. A copy of your insurance policy and your contact details should be kept close at hand.

**11. Local SIM Card: - When you are there, think about getting a local SIM card. This will allow you to stay in touch with your lodging, make local calls, and get in touch with emergency services.

Check with your government or other relevant authorities for any travel advisories or safety suggestions prior to your trip to the Maldives.

Make sure you are familiar with the emergency protocols at your lodging, particularly if you are staying in a remote or local island. It is imperative that you are well-informed and ready to ensure your safety when visiting the Maldives.

helpful people and websites

- Here are a few helpful numbers and links for visitors to the Maldives:
-
- **1. Emergency Services:
-
- Dial 119 for police, ambulance, or fire department emergencies.
- **2. Police for Tourists:
-
- In the Maldives, the Tourist Police may help visitors with a variety of issues. Give them a call at +960 969 6006.
- **3. National Defense Force of the Maldives (MNDF):
-

- **4. **Maldives Immigration: Call the MNDF at 191 for assistance with water-related emergencies and maritime search and rescue activities.
-
- Website: Immigration to the Maldives
- for more on immigration issues, admission criteria, and visas.
- **5. Customs Service in the Maldives:
-
- Visit the Maldives Customs website for details on rules and practices pertaining to customs.6. Airports Company Limited in the Maldives (MACL):
-
- Maldives Airports website
- **7. Maldives Meteorological Service: For details on airports in the Maldives, such as Velana International Airport
-
- Maldives Meteorological Service website
- Regarding meteorological predictions and updates. **8. Dhivehi Red Crescent:
-

- Dhivehi Red Crescent website
- For details regarding emergency response and medical assistance.9. Monetary Authority of the Maldives (MMA):
-
- Visit the Maldives Monetary Authority website for details on money and banking issues.
- **10. **Language: Divehi Website: Dhivehi Bas - Learn the fundamentals and phrases of Dhivehi online.
-
- **11. **Maldives Tourism: Visit Maldives is the official tourism website that offers details on resorts, things to do, and advice on traveling.
-
- **12. **Advisories for Travel: - For the most recent information and safety advice for visiting the Maldives, see the travel advisory website of your government.
-
- **13. **Related SIM Card Vendors:
- Chiraagu: Chiraagu

- - Ooredoo: Madeira Ooredoo

For visitors to the Maldives, these contacts and websites provide a variety of necessary services and information. Prior to and throughout your journey, always make sure you have the most recent contact information.

Conclusion

Discovering the Maldives presents an unparalleled and remarkable encounter brimming with scenic splendor, vivacious aquatic life, and an opulent cultural legacy. Here are some parting thoughts and words of wisdom to motivate your trip to the Maldives:

**1. Earthly paradise:
Overwater villas, immaculate white sand beaches, and glistening blue waters are the Maldives' most well-known features. It is a veritable heaven on Earth, providing a serene and beautiful environment for rest and renewal.

**2. Wonderland Underwater:
Take in the stunning underwater scenery of the Maldives. The coral reefs are brimming with vibrant fish, sharks, rays, and other marine life, whether you're diving, snorkeling, or going on an underwater adventure.

**3. Diversity of Cultures:

The Maldives are known for more than just their breathtaking natural beauty. Discover nearby islands, take in traditional dances and music, and taste the distinctive flavors of Maldivian food.

**4. Kind Hospitality

The inhabitants of the Maldives are renowned for their kind disposition and gracious hospitality. You'll be welcomed with open arms and sincere grins as soon as you arrive.

**5. Adventure Is Waiting:

Whether you want to unwind on the beach, experience exhilarating water sports, or go island hopping, the Maldives has a wide variety of activities to choose from.

**6. Ecotourism:

The Maldives is dedicated to eco-friendly travel methods. The delicate island ecosystem is the subject of numerous resorts and municipal activities aimed at conserving the environment.

**7. Romantic Getaways:

The Maldives is a well-liked location for honeymoons and romantic trips because of its overwater villas, exclusive dining options, and stunning sunsets.

**8. Memorable Dawns and Sunsets:

**9. Island Hopping Adventures: - Take in the breathtaking sunsets and sunrises over the Indian Ocean, which will leave you in awe and at ease long after you depart. Discover the various Maldivian atolls and islands, each with a distinct charm and personality. Explore regional markets, cultural events, and off-the-beaten-path hidden treasures.

**10. Make Everlasting Memories: - Whether you're looking to celebrate a special event, go on an adventure, or just relax in paradise, the Maldives offer the ideal setting for making lifelong memories.

**11. A Genuine Getaway: - The Maldives provides a genuine getaway from the daily grind.

Take some time to unplug from technology, get outside, and take in some quiet time.

**12. Accept the Maldivian Spirit: - Accept the carefree Maldivian spirit, where time appears to stand still and the allure of the islands beckons you to savor life's small pleasures.

Discover a place in the Maldives that goes beyond the picture-perfect scenery, providing a deep connection to nature and an unwinding atmosphere that will linger long. The Maldives extends a warm welcome to everyone seeking a genuinely remarkable and remarkable experience, be they a family seeking adventure, a couple seeking romance, or a solitary traveler seeking solitude. So gather your belongings, set out on this tropical journey, and allow the breathtaking Maldivian scenery to enchant you. Happy travels!

Printed in Great Britain
by Amazon